"... NO ONE

has the right to equate Christianity with weakness or to imagine that the Bible teaches us always to surrender. The biblical message proclaims the sovereign greatness of God which transcends all lesser principles or standards which we might wish to draw from it . . . .

"Man's great temptation is to want to know by himself what is good and what is evil. He wants to know whether he should withstand or not, but without needing any counsel from God. . . . What is good, in the Bible, is not this thing or that. It is not a matter of resisting or giving in. It is doing what God wants and when he wants it; it is total dependence upon his person, not upon a moral code."

PAUL TOURNIER is a Swiss physician whose interest in the whole man led him to the practice of psychotherapy. He has made a significant contribution to our understanding of modern psychology and its relation to the Christian faith. His books have been translated into ten languages. Among his other titles are *The Meaning of Gifts, To Understand Each Other, Secrets,* and *The Seasons of Life.*

TO RESIST OR
TO SURRENDER?

by Paul Tournier

Translated by John S. Gilmour

JOHN KNOX PRESS Atlanta

The German original edition was published under the title: *Sich Durchsetzen oder Nachgeben* by Rascher Verlag, Zürich.

This translation was made from *Tenir tête ou céder*, published in 1962 by Éditions Labor et Fides, Geneva.

The Scripture quotations in this book are from the Revised Standard Version of the Bible, copyrighted 1946 and 1952 by the Division of Christian Education, National Council of the Churches of Christ in the United States of America.

Published by Pillar Books for John Knox Press
International Standard Book Number: 0-8042-3663-1
Library of Congress Catalog Card Number: 64-16284

© M.E. Bratcher 1964

First mass paperback edition 1976

Printed in the United States of America

TO RESIST OR
TO SURRENDER?

I. THE TROUBLED WORLD AND THE CHURCH

DURING THE WAR a young German theologian, Dr. Eberhard Müller, was serving as chaplain on the distant Russian steppes. His thoughts turned often to the days ahead. He clearly foresaw the catastrophe to which the mad adventure of the Third Reich was heading. But what after that? Who could rise up from the ruins? What could he himself do for his country? He was not so much concerned with the political or military aspect of his people's destiny as with the moral. His nation had been poisoned by Nazi ideology. It had penetrated into all the areas of professional and social life, especially among the younger people. Teachers had to inculcate it; jurists and physicians had to apply its laws, directly destroying the dignity of men. Who could straighten out such disorder in so many minds?

No one but the church, of course. Had she not received God's revelation in order to make it the basis of social life? But the church herself was not blameless of responsibility for what had happened: Had she not, for centuries already, withdrawn from the concrete problems of the world? What had she done to help solve the tragedy and shame of German unemployment, for example, which had served the Nazis as a springboard to power? Was it so strange that a false prophet should arise, claiming to hold the answer?

It was therefore necessary, if the church were to assume her task in the face of such profound disorder in the world, that she come out of sheltered retreat where she had withdrawn. She would have to come out of her chapels in order to meet the people where they are, bringing understanding to their problems and help in solving them. She could no longer be content with preaching to devoted and convinced followers once a week. Nor could she be satisfied just to preach salvation, conversion, and the great Christian doctrines.

She would have to take up those problems which men meet every day in their work, be they jurists, doctors, teachers, merchants, housewives, politicians, technicians, artists, peasants, or whatever. First, she needed to find out what their problems were. Was the church aware of the world's problems? Pastors study theology, but what was needed now was a continuing dialogue wherein theologians meet men and women from all walks of life in order to study with them their difficulties in life behavior and in what way Christian faith could help them work these out.

Toward the end of the war, Dr. Müller spoke of this to Bishop Wurm, and with the latter's support founded the first Evangelical Academy in Germany, at Bad Boll. The first session took place in September 1945. It was a session for jurists. There, face to face, were judges who had held out during the Nazi era and judges who had given in; the former had, in fact, resigned rather than be forced to act against their conscience. The latter had refused resignation as a cowardly way out, and in line with our modern principle of the separation of powers, had stayed at their post. After all, a judge's task is to apply the law, not to question the morality of the law at the bar of personal conscience.

How complex are the problems of this world! And how hard it is to draw from Christian faith concrete answers to those concrete problems which the working world poses daily. This is what the Evangelical Academies discovered in every session. Along with my wife, I took part in the first medical session at Bad Boll, in May 1946. That experience had a great influence upon my life.

For ten years I had felt called to concentrate my study upon the role of spiritual life in the health of men. But up until this time I had been very much alone. Then at Bad Boll, in a country torn apart by war, I discovered that the most learned medical men were very much concerned with this same relationship, even those who up until then had had virtually no contact with the church. Enlightened by what had taken place in their land, they now realized that their profession had paid too great a price for having forgotten its priestly origins, for having become secular, detached from all religious or philosophical reference in order to obey only science and technique. Was it not in the name of science and progress that doctors had let themselves be drawn into criminal acts? Neither science nor technique could give the doctors an adequate or whole view of the human person. Reduced to the elements of science and technique, medicine was in danger of losing its human quality, of becoming dangerously impersonal.

The same problems are true for every other profession. Evangelical Academies have sprung up all over Germany, and similar attempts to achieve an on-going dialogue between the church and the various human disciplines have been made in many other countries. At Bad Boll I have taken part in sessions for artists, engineers, architects, nurses, businessmen, and also for the leaders of industry. The present-day crisis of Western civilization reaches down equally into every sector of social life, for our civilization has been cut off from its spiritual sources.

It is a striking fact that the various professions are

far less separated by their specialization than what we have thought. It gives us hope that our modern world may be able to rediscover that which is truly human, beyond our technical compartmentalizing, once we begin to think a bit more about life, rather than simply react to it. There are certain questions which face every sector of society. This I hope to demonstrate by studying one of these questions: "To resist or to surrender?"

It may astonish some that I, a doctor, should write upon such a problem, expressed to me by responsible economists meeting together to discuss a very technical question, that of the consequences of the present tendency of private property to become ever more diffuse in its ownership. Yet our differing disciplines will ever more greatly be influencing each other. For philosophy has been shaken by physics, medicine has served to renew pastoral care, the automobile industry has transformed town-planning, architecture has modified the housekeeper's life, the radio and TV have changed the face of politics, chemical industry has completely changed our textiles, and mechanics is in the process of doing the same to agriculture. Mr. Louis Armand,* a famous engineer, recently stated that there are so many human problems created by technical progress that the great industrial firms will, in the future, have to have a collective leadership, wherein psychologists and moralists will have their necessary place alongside technical experts and economists.

It is time for us to come out of the prison of specialization and to establish a dialogue, not just between the church and the professions but among the professions themselves. We need to face, on a larger scale, those questions which cannot be answered from within a single profession. This is essential to the recovery of the truly human. Who knows but one day it may well be our poets who come to the rescue of our engineers!

*Louis Armand and Michel Drancourt, *Plaidoyer pour l'avenir* (Paris: Calmann-Lévy, 1961).

II. TO RESIST OR TO SURRENDER? THAT IS OUR QUESTION

I HAVE BEEN extremely interested in studying this difficult question. I quickly saw that it applies to all relationships between men, to all their tactics, and to all their conflicts. What is it that makes an individual or a group decide to impose its will upon another and the other to give in? Or both to hold off each other in unceasing struggle? Are they aware themselves of the reason?

For two months I questioned many men and women of various backgrounds and types of work. Generally, the people I questioned were quite surprised at first. They seemed never to have asked themselves the question, even though several times throughout every day of their lives they had had to decide whether or not they would give in to certain demands. Then they grew thoughtful; they began to recall particularly decisive moments when they had had to take a stand. Sometimes they had been carried along by a power which surprised them to a victory equally surprising. Other times they had given in against their inner convictions and without knowing why. Occasionally they may have long remained painfully perplexed before being obliged to decide, and even now they are not very sure of what

13

had made them decide for or against, nor whether their decision was right.

Whether it is a farmer selling a cow at the fair or two theologians discussing doctrine, an adolescent who is trying to extract a privilege from his unwilling parents or diplomats who are negotiating war or peace, there are always two interests, two convictions, and in the last analysis, two wills which confront each other.

I am not suggesting that the subject of the conflict is unimportant. On the contrary, the more serious the issue the more stirred up are the passions. This is the origin of the famous expression *rabies theologica:* theological madness. But what we can clearly state is that the same psychological mechanisms work in all these situations, mechanisms which are extremely subtle and complex, partly conscious and partly unconscious. It is they which determine the outcome of the debate.

It is not always the strong who win, as the realists imagine. Nor is it always those whose argument is the most reasonable, as idealists would think. It is a well-known fact that little dogs bark much more than big ones, and sometimes scare them off by sheer noise. The strong can afford to give in majestically, for they have no need of victory in order to gain prestige; the weak become desperately obstinate in order to reassure themselves. They will argue against plain logic and even against their interests, because they cannot stand being defeated.

A certain man had been for a long time in conflict with his in-laws who have greatly humiliated him. Upon another affront he broke with them. Friends tried to intervene: Could he not make a gesture toward conciliation by agreeing to see them again? No, it would mean avoiding the problem, he replied, not solving it. Nothing would be changed; they would simply close their eyes again to a difference of conviction which they had not wished to recognize, except now when he has openly broken off.

By nature peaceful and kind, he is far more desirous of good relations with everyone than he is of disputes. Yet, surprisingly, he becomes unyielding. "I would gladly give in if it were only my interests involved," he reasons, "but I bear the burden of others' interests as well, and it would be treason to sacrifice them for my selfish desire for peace." And he repeats, with some guilty feelings, the old adage which he really abhors: *si vis pacem, para bellum.*

Often thus, wise and thoughtful men are suddenly surprised by conflicts into which they are dragged, conflicts they neither foresaw nor desired. A strange chain of events makes them, in spite of themselves, leaders of a resistance which they are no longer free to leave. Their followers would not allow them to: they could well repeat the famous saying, "I am their chief; I am obliged to follow."

When I was a member of the governing body of my church, I found myself in serious conflict with my own pastor, the very one whom I admired and loved most of all in the whole Assembly. We had unwittingly been pitted one against the other. Those who feared his ideas lined up with me and encouraged me on to combat him. Those who feared mine similarly pushed him on to the fight against me. Neither of us thus could give in without disappointing all those who had trusted us.

Following a profound spiritual experience, we found ourselves back together again, on our knees, in his office. We admitted how greatly we had both suffered, how much we still admired one another, and we asked each other for forgiveness for the cruel words which in the disagreement we had allowed ourselves to pronounce. I shall never forget that reconciliation, nor shall I forget the price it cost in terms of pride.

A while back I spoke of Bishop Wurm, one of the leaders in the Confessing Church, who so heroically stood up to Hitler in Nazi Germany. Shortly after the war, when I was asking him about that tragic era, he told me how hard it had been, at the beginning of Hitler's reign, to know what attitude the church should take. There was a tremendous, popular movement whipping up the enthusiasm of the masses for new hope. Should the church step in line, in spite of the movement's obvious flaws, in the hope of influencing the new regime and of directing it toward a true national renewal? Or must the church fight the regime, thus losing all contact with the masses? True, the new leaders committed grave injustices, and professed doctrines quite contrary to Christian faith. But was this not the case of most political leaders, at least to some degree? Complete withdrawal may be taken either as an act of courage or surrender.

Resist or surrender: Which should they do? Bishop Wurm discussed this often with a close friend, a fellow bishop, who was equally hesitant. Then one night Bishop Wurm suddenly felt called by God to break with the regime. He immediately obeyed the divine call. Happily so, for he was but a hair breadth from becoming inextricably involved, through compromise upon compromise, to the point where he never could have stopped. Thus these two close friends, having long hesitated together, became the leaders of the two factions in the church which became irreconcilably opposed to each other, one in resistance and the other in subjection.

III. DETERMINISMS

THUS THERE ALWAYS enters into every conflict a terrible, vicious circle: he who does not stand up in time is carried forward into ceaseless compromise right on to final capitulation. Conversely, he who does not offer to compromise, in time, is forced to harden his attitude even more, often even against his own convictions.

Instead of asking, "Shall I resist or shall I give in?" we should sometimes ask ourselves a much more penetrating question. "If I give in, is it willingly, or against my desires? If I hold out, is it out of conviction, or not?" Even so, it is often most difficult for us to answer these questions with certainty. How many people there are, many of the most capable, who remain perplexed and who, once their decision is made, cannot tell if it was freely made or if they were moved by unconscious motives.

A man may believe himself most completely disinterested in a cause for which he is fighting. Thus he keeps his conscience clear, whereas in fact it is his will to conquer that drives him on. A woman who always was forced to give in to her husband, to take another example, suddenly shows herself to be invincible when

17

he begins to lord it over the children. She discovers in herself an energy unknown before, when it becomes a matter of defending the children rather than herself. Yet, in reality, it is a type of personal revenge which she is taking out for her past humiliations.

Thus in the most common of marital struggles we may isolate those factors which are present in every clash: of different social classes or generations, of political parties, of nations, of scientists, artists, or philosophers. Let us not imagine it otherwise in economic conflicts or in money matters. The object may be very material, but the clash is always spiritual. In demanding higher wages, for instance, or even in the common bargaining over a price, it is a question of winning justice, a fair deal, and respect for one's person by the other partner.

Or let us consider the great industrialist always complaining of the overwork his business imposes upon him. He sets out to enlarge his factory, to open new branches, and to take over competing businesses. It is not money that he is after, for he hasn't any time to take a vacation or to enjoy the money he already has. He is simply obeying nature's law which requires every organism to keep developing. He who does not go forward falls behind. Life itself is nothing else but the totality of so many biological victories over the continual forces of death.

Life is the being's affirmation over against its environment which both menaces and supports it. Life is inseparable from conflict. It is amazing that the scientific study of this general psychology of particular conflicts has been so neglected. Perhaps it is because we are involved and therefore find it so hard to see them objectively.

All men are constantly being dragged into countless conflicts which engulf them and make playthings, rather than actors, out of them. All become indignant at and protest the injustices of which they are victims. All equally and unwittingly commit just as many injustices and wrongs upon others.

Their arguments intersect but never answer each other. As far as it is possible to understand them dispassionately, we generally must admit that each is right, from his own point of view. This is what I find so often in my practice when I listen to husband and wife, in turn, in their conflict.

Each of us, to be sure, believes he is only defending sacred principles such as truth, fairness, and reason. It is only in others that we discern self-interest, passion, and sophism leading them on. This is why discussion so rarely can convince anyone. In all my life I can remember only one argument which really changed my mind. Political men know this, for they count far more on the power of suggestion in a few well-hammered slogans than in any rational argumentation.

Yet everyone continues unceasingly to argue, to put forth his logical reasonings which by-pass those of others to no avail. What joy people get when they discover some line of argument which appears irrefutable. They arouse the applause of their partisans who see in them already a decisive victory. But they are always disappointed and angered by the opponent's reaction, because a knock-out argument stimulates his ability to parry and awakens in him an abundance of arguments for the contrary. These are even more vigorous, which he in turn brandishes triumphantly, with no thought of refuting the argument just put to him.

Reason in no way directs men as it used to be believed. The analyses of historians, economists, Marxists, existentialists, and psychoanalysts have forever cured us of that illusion. Reason serves only to justify, within the field of full consciousness, the behavior which obscure natural forces dictate to us, forces such as the instinct of preservation, of possession or of aggressiveness, of sexual desire, or the instincts for power or for fulfillment.

Every school explains human behavior in its own
way. Marxists see only the effects of economic and social structures; psychoanalysts see the effects of unconscious drives; while idealists see those of moral conscience, described in philosophical or religious terms.
Actually, every attitude is the result of a great number
of extremely complex factors. Every human relationship is an equilibrium of meeting forces, a more or less
stable balance, a struggle, until one of the two individuals or groups gives in, surrenders to the other.

Zuckermann* studied the social life of monkeys. He
showed that in a colony of monkeys there reigns a certain degree of harmony as long as one of the old monkeys maintains sufficient authority for no other to dare
oppose him. However, the instant he is obliged to step
down before another's challenge, a period of instability
sets in all through the colony. This changes only when
one of the males succeeds in establishing his mastery
over all. Even among monkeys it is doubtful that physical strength is the sole determinant. The ruling mon-
key relies upon a certain degree of self-confidence and
courage which depend upon emotional strength.
Among men, of course, the composing elements are
much more subtle, complex, and varied. There enters
into the scene not just physical and emotional strength,
but spiritual factors as well. But once again there is the
equilibrium of forces which will determine one of the
partners giving in.

*Dr. S. Zuckermann, *La vie sexuelle et sociale des singes.* Translated
from English by A. Petitjean, NRF, Gallimard, Paris.

IV. TO EACH HIS WEAPONS

EACH OF US uses the weapons which he has at hand. For one it is physical strength, while for another it is precisely his weakness, a kind of extortion through appeal to his weakness, to the other's sensitivity, to despair. Many neuroses and illnesses, more or less consciously cultivated, serve as weapons by which things otherwise unobtainable are brought within reach. Impulsiveness serves one, while tenacious obstruction serves another; interminable or eloquent speeches win for some, while others use an obstinate silence.

The same point can repeat itself time after time. The wife excites herself to the point of nervous collapse and threats of suicide while her husband clutches ever more strongly to his most inhuman and exasperating self-mastery. Which of the two is responsible for the other's behavior? There are little words which sting worse than a slap, jokes fuller of venom than any insult.

Moreover, it is possible to gain mastery over another person through generosity and sweetness, quite as much as through open aggression. We see such family situations, completely dominated by the wife, reigning by virtue of her kindness, her scrupulous perfection, and her tender attentions. Everyone admires her self-

21

lessness and holds her to be a model wife and mother, without seeing that she is actually paralyzing her loved ones' personalities. No one would dare hurt her by opposing her or freeing himself from her. The success of this tactic leads her on in the virtuous role she is playing.

On the other hand, there are many who are always upholding love, but upholding it in a very unlovely way, or those who fight for toleration in the most intolerant spirit toward their chosen enemies. Those who cannot threaten seek to trick; those who cannot attack take to flight. But we never know if the one who gives in is not doing so, so as to obtain victory more surely.

Of course, we find all this with a thousand shades of degree in the games of flirtation and love so well studied by our novelists, as well as in business and in artistic or scientific life. Every progress in civilization adds another note to this great organ concert that we all must learn to utilize in social life. Each has his strong points, the prestige of wealth or of impressiveness, school and university successes or sport triumphs. Beauty counts for the woman. For the man, it is his wife's beauty, just as for the wife her husband's reputation.

And there are many surprises! Men obviously strong and brave will, in certain circumstances, suddenly surrender in such a cowardly manner that they are themselves horrified by it. Others who always seem unsure, hesitating, and spineless, may suddenly show themselves in an emergency to be quite capable of unyielding firmness. I find myself to be such a weak person, hesitant and never desirous of taking sides. Yet my friends disagree when I admit this. They consider me a leader. One of them told me the other day, "Yes, of course you may let things go for a long time, but suddenly, once you become convinced of something, you set out to implement it, and no one is able to stop you."

Conflict is much more common today than previously, for social conventions used to settle ahead of time who would win and who would lose, who would order and who would obey. Obviously, marital conflict was much rarer when the woman used to be obliged to submit to her husband. The same was true of the relationship of parents and teen-age children. At the latest Geneva International Conference, when the conditions for happiness were discussed, one session was given over to the problems of young people who felt misunderstood. The secretary noted that misunderstanding explains "both the passivity of a certain segment of youth, those who submit, and the aggressivity of others, those who rebel."

All education implies, sooner or later, conflict between the child and his teacher, no matter how kind the latter may be. Adaptation to society requires many renunciations. It is poor preparation for the child if his teacher gives in easily; yet not to give in means driving him either into rebellion or into neurosis, forced upon him by unyielding authority. He will rebel if he is strong enough; he will become neurotic if he is too weak to free himself. How far must parents resist, and how far dare they give in? Where must the limit be drawn? What parents are there who would claim to have clearly seen all this? Do they even recognize their own behavior? One day my own son threw out at me, "You don't realize that you are far less liberal than you think you are."

There are many parents who do not want to argue with their children for every mistake. They reserve their authority for serious matters. But then it is too late. By forever giving in they lose all authority. Alexis Carrel* has pointed out that most parents give in to their children's whims when they are small, the very age when they need a firm hand. The parents laugh at

*Dr. Alexis Carrel, *Réflexions sur la conduite de la vie* (Paris: Plon, 1950).

their antics then, and later in adolescence try to lay down the law, the very time when children need more freedom in order to gain their own experience.

It soon becomes apparent how great in every age is the question of resisting or surrendering, when we apply it to education in the home, in school, in society. The child's reactions, strong or weak, usually become established and persist throughout all of life. When the child is small, the balance of power is obviously disproportionate. This explains how some are crushed and others are intimidated. Yet we see families wherein a child, usually the youngest, imposes his will on all the others whether he be charming and sweet as an angel or whether he be assertive and unmanageable.

In adolescence the problem comes out in all its sharpness. Parents become accustomed to having to say but a word, or at most to raise the voice a bit, in order to impose their will on their obedient child. This is consoling to them, because outside of their home they are obliged so often to give in to the will of others more powerful than they. Thus it is most shocking and disconcerting to them when the change comes; that this child, so young and small in their eyes, dares to argue back with them is to them an affront and an intolerable defiance.

This upset in the balance of power affects the entire family, which enters into a period of instability similar to that among colonies of monkeys as described by Zuckermann. Yet, these parents must not cowardly abdicate their authority. Youths who win their independence too easily, without having had to wrest it from their resisting parents, are very poorly prepared to make use of it in life. In the struggle the child will acquire experience; he will learn how far he may resist and at what point he must submit.

Similar problems are found in every office and shop, in all businesses and laboratories. A particular balance of power is always established which regulates the relation between various members of the working group and which is upset by the arrival or departure of any new member. Sometimes the head men are too particular and break their men's initiative. Sometimes, on the other hand, they are too weak, so that anarchy reigns. Sometimes they err in both ways, going from one extreme to the other.

Gravest of all is the situation wherein a head man demands an employee's complicity in a dishonest deal, something irregular or immoral. How far can the latter give in, against his own conscience? After all, it is not his business, but his boss's. He is not responsible for straightening out every wrong. And yet, all such fine people who passively stand by when evil is let loose in our world, claiming that it is not their affair, are nevertheless somewhat responsible.

These questions of conscience are very delicate and hard to resolve. I have seen many employees burdened thus for years. I really don't know how to advise them. Should they approach their boss openly and threaten to resign? What if he accepted it rather than change any of his wrong dealings? By what right can employees set themselves up as judge? It is quite possible for one to believe a transaction dishonest, when in reality it is not. It is also possible for the employer's misdeeds, known by all but denounced by none, to poison the whole atmosphere of a business.

Then there is the injustice of the state, of its policy of prestige and of war! How far does the prophet's duty of intransigence go? How far does his duty of surrender to national unity go? We know how tragically such conflicts of conscience can tear apart the most clear-sighted men. I remember a friend who was in charge of a province of his homeland during the German occupation. He did everything in his power to lessen the sufferings of his compatriots during the occupation, to save them, insofar as it was possible, from the application of the most iniquitous orders.

One day he could take no more. Courageously, he decided to go and see the head occupation authority, and to use whatever prestige he still had to extort the promise that he would not be replaced by a Nazi after his resignation. And then, after his resignation, a Nazi was appointed in his place, a docile tool in the hands of the enemy. Did my friend betray his own people by obeying his conscience? Tormented by such questioning, he came to see me. What could I tell him? I could only share his anguish.

Here we can see how vain it would be to try to separate the theoretical aspect of our problem from the practical, that is, the inner decision to resist or to surrender, on the one hand, and the real means which we have at hand with which to impose our will and seize the victory.

What strikes me very much is the emptiness of so many victories in social life won after so much struggle and effort. Men can fight for years for a cause dear to their hearts; they can bravely stand up to the whole world. Yet, when they win their point, their joy is short-lived. The battle gave them energy which they no longer possess. And then, when we get what we want, we no longer can complain. Complaining is one way of throwing responsibility upon others for one's own vexations.

Even the most dearly paid-for military victories rarely bring an enduring settlement. Thus it may seem that all the problems are solved with victory, when, in reality, victory only ushers in new problems vastly more complex than those of war. Again, it is true for us all that victory makes us feel much more sharply what we lack still in order to be all-powerful!

What men hunger for most is to be loved. Herein lies the deepest source of their self-assertive behavior which sets them against each other. This is the tragic paradox in our human situation. If we carefully observe the tritest of marriage disputes, we discover that the partner who obstinately fights on and wants, at any price, to obtain the other's giving in, is really seeking in such surrender a sign of the other's love.

The same is true of the greatest social and political conflicts. The strongest motivation in every movement for social change is the desire to be recognized, respected, and, in the last analysis, to be loved. What sets man against man is their mutual need to be united. A nation which feels itself disliked by its neighbors can throw itself into war as if to oblige such a love which was not forthcoming in peacetime. Thus the rejoicing in alliances formed between nations or individuals who find themselves friends, because they have a common enemy. Just as they join hands in combat, they promptly separate after victory. Victory brings only solitude and ingratitude from those it has profited.

V. INTERPRETATIONS

IMAGINE A WIFE, soon after marrying, discovering that her husband is still attracted to another woman whom he has known before. What can she do? Try to win him over by love, pardon, trust? Demand a choice from him? He is probably a weakling, incapable of making a manly choice. He denies whatever he can; he admits all only when the evidence forces him to it; he promises everything when he's backed into a corner, but he continues his double game afterward. There are many such men, somewhat childish, ready to pluck whatever pleasures in life they can without assuming responsibility. They never have enough women to coddle them.

What then shall his wife do? Forgive him, trust him? Would that not be tantamount to encouraging him in his way of least resistance? However, by leaving him, by turning him out, would she not risk seeing the father of her own children going from dereliction to dereliction, having a very bad influence upon them? A fervent believer, she courageously chooses the path of self-effacement in order to preserve her home and to uphold her husband.

The years pass by and the children reach adolescence. In their teenage absolutism they condemn and despise their father. But they also reproach their mother most severely: by her weakness, say they, she has become an accomplice to the undermining of their home; she is every bit as guilty as their father for the heavy, stifling atmosphere which has characterized their home life.

The mother is overwhelmed. "I have been wrong," she thinks; "I have made a grave mistake; I have made both my husband and my children unhappy! I have been a coward!" Yet it was in complete sincerity that she had first chosen the attitude of forgiveness and perseverance as the more generous, courageous, and constructive way, and as the most faithful way to her God.

Thus it is that the same behavior can be interpreted either as heroic obedience or as shameful surrender! We are not discussing human conduct now—not even our own—but our interpretation of that conduct. Surrender seems to be at times a victory for our affections, or again as a defeat of our thinking. Resistance, as well can appear as courageous victory or as a moral defeat.

Everyone senses that the interpretation, not the act itself, is what counts. Hence our continual anxiety over the interpretation that will be given to our behavior. For example, we fear lest a concession on our part be taken as a sign of weakness by the other party, which would only incite him to be more obstinate than ever. Or again, and this is more subtle, we also are afraid that our intransigence be seen as a sign of weakness, as an act of desperation, to which he might be tempted to give the *coupe de grâce* by adamant resistance.

Such maneuverings are read of daily in the newspapers whenever a group or a nation is conducting difficult negotiations with another. We soon become aware that the negotiators, who well know their opponents, could easily work out some formula of agreement with them, if they did not fear the reactions of their own followers. No individual, and certainly no nation, sees his rivals as they are, but rather as he has been taught to see them and to interpret their conduct.

When we admire somebody, we describe his firmness as bravery and exemplary faithfulness. If we do not like him, however, we see in the same firmness only stupid thick-headedness and sinful pride. He who gives in can in the same way be judged as a coward and a traitor or as a prodigy in nobleness of soul. Where distrust reigns between two men or two groups, the spontaneous gesture of conciliation which one may make, out of genuine open-heartedness, is likely to be received as some Machiavellian trap.

Let us now try to see more clearly those things which make a man oppose or give in to his partner. I questioned a lawyer, a fervent Christian and apostle of nonviolence, counsel for a large insurance firm. Among the accidents, a certain proportion are quite disputable; the responsibilities of the two parties are open to debate. In order to make a friendly settlement, it is essential to make concessions and often to settle for a rather degrading type of "horse trading."

"What makes you decide," I asked, "to hold out, to give in, to compromise, or go to court?" "Basically," he replied, "it is always an appreciation as exact as possible of the chances of losing more or of gaining more." "Then moral values never enter into the question?" I asked. "Of course they do," he retorted. "At times we hold back from taking too much advantage of a situation, where legally all is in our favor. Our hardness could be interpreted as exploitation and could harm our good name." Upon further thought, even this moral scruple seems dictated by self-interest, at least in part.

Our question then has been put off but not answered: What are, in fact, the factors which enter into this game of evaluating risks of loss and chances of gain alluded to above? The main factor, it seems to me, is the natural temperament of each man. There are those who are spontaneously inclined toward fighting and others toward peacemaking. Each will justify his natural impulse by interpreting the situation differently. The former will proclaim his confidence of obtaining substantial advantages, through going to court, which it would be criminal to give up. The other will count out the risks involved and will advise a prudent compromise so as to lessen the damages.

I have already described this diversity in our natural reactions in my book *The Strong and the Weak*. I see ever more clearly in what large measure even the most thoughtful of men are controlled by their automatic impulses. Also, I see how the facts usually uphold their actions. The optimist throws himself with such enthusiasm and confidence into his case that he wins, whereas the timid, who is half-beaten before he starts, would likely lose. Still on the subject of insurance, any company well knows from which doctor it should ask for a particular counsel. It can pretty well foresee which one will give a report most favorable to its interests. The doctor's professional ability, good faith, and impartiality are in no way implicated in what I say here; it is a question of his mental habits, his particular way of looking at things.

In the same way, my attitude toward patients is determined by my temperament. I dislike giving them advice; I am inclined to let them have their own experiences, even bad ones. If there is one who needs a firmer hand, I feel I must send him to a colleague whose nature is quite different from mine. For the patient, I represent the understanding father; my colleague is the strict father; both qualities are equally essential, yet rarely combined in the same person.

I like to think that God can use my colleague and me, as we complement one another, in order to fulfill his plan. I believe that it is for this very reason that he made us so different and entrusted us with the same patient. This is an act of faith which frees me from the anguish of making my choice: now I can freely choose according to my own temperament. It is only by acting in such accord that I can render those services which God expects of me. I will be of help to a client through my understanding, my patience, my tendency to put great trust in him. Another doctor, on the other hand, will be of help through his strictness and the vigorous challenges he will throw out—all of which would sound strange coming from me.

Similarly with regard to medical care, every physician treats his patients according to his own temperament. One doctor may be aggressive, direct, a go-getter; he intervenes immediately and continually, either with the bistoury knife or with countless medications, all as strong as possible. If any one of them should bring some unfortunate reaction, he adds yet another in order to correct it. And he imposes a severe diet with very detailed instructions. Another doctor will be quite cautious; he considers every risk involved in an operation or in a given treatment. He prescribes little, and leaves much to nature. If his patient suggests a treatment which has worked well with one of his friends, this physician will reply that opinions are quite divided about it and that it is wise to avoid it.

The same thing is true of preachers: some will simplify matters, eloquently contrasting faith with doubt, virtue with sin, and the Christian life with worldliness. By such shock-treatment preaching they overwhelm strong personalities capable of heroic decision, leading them to radical and healthy choices. Everything, say they, is different in their life from that day on. But there are other souls, scrupulous and meticulous, who are completely crushed by such preaching, and who wonder if they are really converted because they still find in themselves so much sin and so many doubts. Such people would receive help from an understanding counselor, one who would remind them that in the human heart the tares will still remain with the good grain, and that every one of us can only count upon the grace of God, not upon our own virtues. It seems to me that God is pleased to use each of us according to our natural gifts.

In the same way—and please excuse the comparison!—the industrial leader knows how best to use the abilities of his diverse assistants. To a dynamic and aggressive assistant he may confide certain business which will be boldly undertaken. He will be careful not to entrust him with certain other affairs, for he knows him to be incapable of the necessary tact and prudence. The genius of leadership consists precisely in this art of choosing one's assistants according to the needs of the situation, just as an organist arranges his stops according to the need for angels' voices or for thunder.

Most men, in fact, think less often than it seems to them. They are carried away by their passions, a passion for fighting or a passion for peace, a jealousy and a power-hunger, or again timidity and self-distrust. They are sure that they are right—those who would fight just as those who would compromise. The former hardly consult others, and even if they do, they accept with great difficulty any questioning of their behavior. They lack no argument to show us that they are in the right.

Others would like very much to take time to think, but hardly have the time. Often it is they who bear the heaviest responsibilities in this world. This is what decided my colleague in Paris, Dr. Gros, to give up his medical practice and to dedicate himself to helping the great industrial leaders in the role of a "teacher of how to think," as he calls it. He noticed how much this world's leaders are alone, deprived of partnership by which they might enter into true dialogue and weigh the grave decisions they are forced to make. Between their adversaries' running them down and their supporters' flattery, they do not know to whom they may turn for objective debate on their problems. These problems they need to grasp thoroughly, rather than be forced to daily improvisations and emergency measures.

VI. PERPLEXITIES

THERE ARE, however, many men who think deeply, who want to think and to take all the time and trouble essential to it. Is not man's nobility his power to go beyond his natural reflexes, to a certain degree, so as to make his own decision? It is for such men that this book is intended. They are wondering whether or not any clear standards for life's conduct can really be found in science, psychology, psychoanalysis, philosophy, or theology.

First of all they ask themselves if really free choices are possible. Doctors who adhere to the Pavlovian school do not believe so. They do not contest the sincerity of a man when he judges things according to his conscience. But they hold the conscience itself to have been "conditioned." It is the form in which a man feels all those reflexes elicited from him by his education, his social situation, habit, and all the moral and religious influences, books read and sermons heard, of his life.

Freudian psychoanalysts do not believe in it either, at least not orthodox Freudians. Even though they hold that the goal of analytic therapy is the acquisition of self-direction, their concept of human personality is completely mechanistic and determinist. By their theory of the superego, they reduce every moral ideal to a process of identification. Jungian psychoanalysts admit an ideal of the soul, it is true, inner aspirations of a spiritual order, but these are more ancestral and collective than personal.

The schools of thought have above all shown us that in addition to all those conscious determining factors, there are many others totally or partially unconscious, and very powerful, which contribute toward the automatic and indefinite repetition of the same responses which were emitted during childhood in similar situations. This is as true of the well as it is of the sick. A man rebels against all authority; he is forever fighting and, by his quarrels, sabotaging his own life. It doesn't mean that he is more evil than another. He is simply projecting his continuous Oedipean conflict, the struggle against his father long ago which he was never able to resolve.

One man can always get along well with his subordinates, but never with his superiors. With a second, the situation is just the reverse. Again, another gets along well with women but is always in conflict with men, or vice-versa. A man tyrannizes his wife—and all other women—without realizing at all that he is forever seeking revenge because years before his mother favored his brother over him or because his sister ceaselessly would humiliate him by her cutting mockery. Or another man doing so because his first fiancée shamelessly dropped him for an underhanded rival.

Here is a man who knows well how to defend others, but not himself. At his father's death, he fought through to victory every litigation left unsettled by his father. He identified himself with his father. This was the case, too, when he upheld firmly his mother's cause through painful quarrels in the family. But when it is a question of self-defense, he is paralyzed by emotion, anguished, totally hesitant.

Thus, psychoanalytic therapy can change a man. His conscious control of these unconscious mechanisms can free him from their control. He can affirm himself now whereas he used always to be completely incapable of it. He can defend himself whereas before he never could. But what is tragic is that now he can become a prisoner of the new behavior acquired by his therapy, every bit as much a prisoner as he used to be of his inhibiting complexes. The fear of regression makes him just as incapable of giving in as he used to be of standing up to his opponent.

Like his own psychoanalyst, he will henceforth influence people whom he meets, even without saying anything, and lead them into adopting the same aggressive attitude in life that he has found through therapy. None of us can escape the universal tendency to be drawn along the same way as those people whom we admire, nor to lead those we like very much in our own pathway. A man who consults a twice- or thrice-divorced psychiatrist is on the way to solving his own marital troubles by divorce.

Psychoanalysts criticize me at times for influencing my patients too much, for making them my disciples. I will not argue this. It sometimes happens, as a matter of fact, that a patient, in identifying himself with us, will not only adopt our ideas, but ideas which he thinks are ours. I followed, over a long period of time, the case of a girl living a difficult existence and under intolerable working conditions. When she decided to resign, I was elated. But she was quite astonished at my reaction! She had been expecting my disapproval. In her mind my religious convictions would make me expect her to put up with it all uncomplainingly.

Psychoanalysts also, whether or not they want to, influence their clients every bit as much as I, and sometimes less consciously. Whoever has been psychoanalyzed becomes a disciple and fervent exponent of psychoanalysis. He takes over its language and de-

scribes as "sadist" the person who resists, and "maso-
chist" the one who surrenders. No one escapes these
personal determinisms. This very essay which I am now
writing is being written in my style. Any other man
would write it in a different way.

Thus, the further science progresses the more it reveals both conscious and unconscious factors control-
ling human behavior and influencing our choices. The
more schools of thought, sociological and psychological
theories, observations, and experiments that there are,
the more numerous and powerful do such factors appear; the more man seems to be a kind of puppet,
manipulated by hidden mechanisms.

Must we then conclude that all free choice is impossible? I do not think so. Rather, I believe—and this is
paradoxical in appearance only—that the more a man
becomes aware of the power of both external and internal determinants, the more he comes to experience
freedom. To be sure it is not freedom as people used to
think of it: absolute, stable, sovereign. It is more a
progressive and trial-and-error movement toward
freedom.

It is precisely through critical study of ourselves and
our decisions, through awareness of all the determinants which may well give us the illusion of acting
freely and yet lead us blindly, that we can free ourselves further. Science makes us vigilant; it shows how
great are the rationalizing mechanisms which fool us.
Yet, it is to the degree that we realize their strength
that we are able to free ourselves from them.

It is therefore essential that we warn those who desire to think. Thinking is not easy. It demands brutally
clear thinking about oneself. How hard it is to see
clearly into ourselves or into what is going on in our
mind when we are faced with making a decision! We
can no longer trust reason, as we so unreservedly used
to. Even when we seek advice from others, we cannot

forget the warning from Jean-Paul Sartre: When people choose their counselor, they are already choosing the advice which they want.

The result is often that the more thought we take, the more hesitant we become. Recently here in Geneva there was a debate on the lack of political interest evidenced among intellectuals. A philosopher rightly showed that the more education gives a man liberty in his judgment, the more complex and shaded every issue appears to him. He sees the valid reasons both "for" and "against," and becomes all the more incapable of taking sides, of being mixed up in the argument. Thus those who act are those who think the least, and those who think are those who do the least acting.

In order to avoid this tragic dilemma, many present-day philosophers are trying to combine with their chapters on philosophical reflection others on the problems of our day. Some philosophers have resolutely committed themselves to political action. This course of action has often tempted me, too. However, I am not very sure that it would constitute any more of an active involvement than does my daily work in the consultation room, when I help men to see themselves more clearly and to free themselves from that which is determining their activity.

What is very rare, so much so as to constitute almost a miracle, is to find an authoritarian person giving in, or a weak person resisting. It is just as difficult to help a weak person learn to defend himself as it is to help a strong person to renounce the use of strength. Yet, all of us sense that it is in just such a choice that a man becomes truly a man; what we call a person. It is when he succeeds in passing beyond the determinism of automatic reflexes to accede to a greater freedom.

I cannot really decide whether I should resist or surrender unless I am inwardly just as capable of resistance as I am of giving in. This equal availability of the two lines of behavior is the first condition laid down for serious thinking. It is equally evident that thought alone is not enough for making valid decisions, since our thinking is always influenced by our environment, our past, our prejudices and complexes, and our affinities. Such influences may be recognized by us or may remain quite unknown.

VII. CHRISTIAN PASSIVE RESISTANCE?

IF, THEN, THOUGHT is both so necessary and so difficult and, in any case, never sufficient, can we count on divine guidance? Yes, I believe this. But there again we must realize that it is no easy path. Certainly the attitude of faith is the most favorable one for one's being available, so to speak, to choose either course of action. Surrendering one's life to God means sincerely trying to empty oneself of all self-will, of even prejudice, and of every reaction which is merely "natural." Since we are never entirely free, since we always depend upon someone or something, it is certainly by dependence upon God that we have the means of knowing the greatest possible freedom.

From this point on our problem lies on a different plane. It is no longer a question of selection by virtue of thought and analysis of all our complexes. It is no longer a question of our judging whether we should resist or surrender. It involves knowing if God wants us to resist or surrender. In each particular situation which arises, it becomes a matter of seeking the guidance of God.

But there you are! What is the will of God? Are we not in danger of ascribing to him our own decisions? Is it not by so-called divine inspiration that so many errors and atrocities have been committed down through history? There are no blinder battlers than those who are convinced that God himself has pushed them into it. Nor are there any blinder defeatists than those who believe God himself to be ordering them to surrender.

Theologians warn us of these dangers of illuminism. Hence the search in the Bible for more objective indications of God's will. Unfortunately, however, we all read the Bible through the tinted glasses of our own temperaments. The distressed see only the warnings of eternal punishment and judge themselves to be damned. The careless see only the promises of God's infinite mercy which will look after everything, in the end. The greatest saints projected their complexes into their interpretation of the Bible. Dr. Nodet* has shown this in Saint Jerome, one whose contribution was precisely that of putting the Bible in the place of high honor.

Psychologists see many weak persons who see their weakness as a Christian virtue and who justify it with verses from the Bible. In vain do we show them their apparent sweetness and selflessness as hiding a formidable repressed hostility which they have turned in against themselves. In vain do we reveal to them that the man who fears to express his hatred is also incapable of true love. In vain do we tell them, "Come now, affirm yourself; defend yourself!" These pious clients think of certain Gospel passages which exhort us not to resist evil, to turn the other cheek when we are smitten on one, to offer our tunic to the one who has taken away our coat, and to go the second mile for the man who has forced us to go the first for him (Matt. 5:38-42; Luke 6:27-35).

We could not in honesty gloss over these Bible pas-

*Dr. Charles H. Nodet, *Position de Saint Jérôme en face des problèmes sexuels,* Carmelite Studies, "Mystique et Continence," Desclée de Brouwer, p. 308.

sages, nor many others on the giving up of all possessions, nor the example of Christ himself keeping silence before Pilate and taking the whipping, the taunts, and the insults without a murmur. Then there is the example of the martyrs, and of men like Francis of Assisi who found the pathway of high spiritual life in simplicity, poverty, and passive resistance. All of these are irrefutable.

Paul takes up this idea in his Letter to the Romans (12:17-20), and adds this strange comment: We shall thus heap coals of fire upon the evil man's head. Apparently, this seemingly uncharitable phrase refers to the remorse that our kindness will create in the offender, which may lead him to repentance. In any case, it is the automatic response of revenge which is condemned.

In its critical notes on these texts the *Bible de Jerusalem* says, "Jesus forbids revenge, but not fighting against evil in the world." Very well, but this fails to solve our problem: just think of all the sufferings, unjustly inflicted throughout history, under the pretext of combating evil in the world.

True, vengeance is a horrible, vicious circle. Each victory cries for revenge in the one defeated, such a hardening that it will lead him to commit even worse cruelty. The precept of "eye for an eye" in the Old Testament was a tremendous step forward, by forbidding the infliction of more suffering than one has received. Jesus takes the final step in order to break the fatal determinism in revenge by forbidding the rendering of blow for blow. He adds, "Great will be your reward."

Marxists have accused Christianity of being accomplice to every injustice by promising to all its victims a reward in heaven. But it is very clearly a reward in this world that Christ speaks of, in the texts quoted. It is a joy which can be found here below in not avenging oneself, and a wealth which can be found in sacrificing all. We can see in this joy the effect of being set free from the natural defense mechanism of revenge. "Vengeance is mine, and recompense," says the Lord (Deut. 32:35). Non-vengeance is an act of faith in the justice of God.

The distinction between combat and revenge is therefore very important. It is woven into the fabric of the entire Bible, which is far less concerned with human behavior as such than with the underlying motives of the behavior. In this the Bible is in complete accord with modern psychology which always moves back from the act to the motive. To the question "Should I resist or surrender?" both Bible and psychology answer, "What are your motives for resisting or giving in?" We can fight for revenge or completely apart from revenge; we can also give in for revenge, or apart from revenge.

In this regard we must make another distinction: between nonviolence and surrender. The nonviolence of Ghandi or William Penn is in no way to be mistaken for surrender. The very opposite is true. It is a method, better than violence, by which we can win our enemy to our conviction. This is well illustrated by Ghandi's victory over British imperialism. In our present world, and as often among Christians as among their adversaries, the gospel is all too often mistaken for weakness and surrender. Such interpretation leads many believers into a spirit of abdication, and leads some right to neurosis.

In one of Isaiah's passages, where the Messiah is spoken of, the Servant of the Lord cries out, "I gave my back to the smiters, and my cheeks to those who pulled out the beard . . . I have set my face like a flint" (Isa. 50:6, 7). Here, as in the Passion of Christ, it is clear that the silence under mistreatment is anything but weakness. The expression "like a flint" expresses this truth eloquently. None was more heroic than Jesus. The Bible shows him as the "fighter par excellence," the one who takes on Satan, the powers of this world, and even his own misguided loved ones: his mother, and his friends like Peter when the latter would try to dissuade him from the cross. He speaks of the strife that his own person will create: "I am come to set a fire upon the earth." Never once does he retreat one inch under the attacks of the Pharisees. In another setting we see him brandishing a whip.

Faith always raises up strong personalities, who do not fear even combat with God: Jacob, for instance. "You have striven with God," said the angel, "and with men, and have prevailed" (Gen. 32:23-32). And to Gideon, who doubts both himself and the miracles he sees: "Go in this might of yours . . ." (Judg. 6:14). There is Amos, the small shepherd, who stands up to the king and all his court; there are all the prophets every one of whom stands up for God and will not be put off! The same Peter who gave in to the point of denial under a servant girl's questions later stood up to the whole Sanhedrin and boldly declared, "We must obey God rather than men" (Acts 5:29). Then there is Paul who, when the "strategists" in Macedonia would let him out of prison "through the back door," cries out boldly, "They have beaten us publicly, uncondemned, men who are Roman citizens, and have thrown us into prison; and do they now cast us out secretly? No! let them come themselves and take us out" (Acts 16:37). Paul also refers to the way in which he withstood Peter over the Jewish-Gentile controversy (Gal. 2:11). We would have to add the whole of Christian history, its martyrs, its saints, including even gentle Francis of Assisi who stood up to his father, and later on, to his pope.

What then may we conclude? That everyone can

quote biblical texts to justify his behavior and his reactions? In any case, no one has the right to equate Christianity with weakness or to imagine that the Bible teaches us always to surrender. The biblical message proclaims the sovereign greatness of God which transcends all lesser principles or standards which we might wish to draw from it. What is good, in the Bible, is not this thing or that. It is not a matter of resisting or giving in. It is doing what God wants and when he wants it: it is total dependence upon his person, not upon a moral code. The story of the Fall is very clear: Man's great temptation is to want to know by himself what is good and what is evil. He wants to know whether he should withstand or not, but without needing any counsel from God. To the horror of many a pious soul, our Bible is filled with divinely ordered wars and skir-

VIII. DIVINE INSPIRATION

FOLLOWING UPON the demise of human reason is that of morality, even that of a moral system supposedly drawn from the Bible. Who can teach us in every circumstance whether we are to resist or to surrender? Only God. Reason, science, psychology, ethics, and theology can help us, but only up to a point and always subordinated to God. We cannot escape the difficulty of this question which keeps arising. It would mean, among other things, seeking to escape from responsibility to God. We are responsible for our obedience, even though in each concrete situation it may be so hard to know what his will is. This is the paradox of our human existence, from which there is no escape.

Can we, then, count upon direct inspiration from God? Yes, I believe so. I am always at a loss to understand those Christians who deny this. The Bible is full of examples, from Abram's call to leave his homeland, Moses' call before the burning bush, the signs in the heaven and the law's reception in Sinai, the calls to all the prophets wherein God told them what they were to do and say, all the way to the gospel and apostolic writings. There we see the calm certainty of Jesus who is led by his Father, Joseph and Paul who are warned by God through dreams . . . there is finally the experience of believers all through the ages including our own days.

Yes, I believe that this search for direct guidance from God is the path of greatest freedom. However, even here our old difficulties reappear. I shall always remember Rev. Mr. Shoemaker, of New York, as he shouted out in his strong voice, "When we find a closed door, we must always ask ourselves if God wants to stop us, or if He is forcing us to break our way through."

But how can we know? It is not easy and we often err. Neither our biblical knowledge nor our wisest counselor, nor even a psychotherapist, when he is able to help us see our way, can spare us the need to perceive for ourselves the voice of God, which may be in a verse of Scripture, or in a wise word of counsel. Nor can we wait, so as to be completely sure of having heard God's voice, before obeying, for it is through our acts of disobedience that we gradually learn to discern God's leading. Further, and despite all our mistakes, there is no more fruitful way than that of trusting in the leading of God's spirit.

Indeed, I have seen men whose every natural defense mechanism led them to fight, and who suddenly and miraculously have given in. This is under divine intervention. And others whose natural determinism led them to surrender, who have by divine inspiration become unyielding. These decisions have been followed by great developments, precisely because they were supernatural. A word of direction received in our time of quietness before God can often direct us better than our wisest reasoning.

Such is true not only in so-called spiritual matters, as is more readily admitted, but also in the most down-to-earth and concrete problems. God makes no division in our problems. I well remember a financial dispute which I once had with a very eminent banking official. It was my only such experience; I felt sure that I was in the right, but he possessed powerful means of putting pressure on me. I offered to meet him in the presence of a notary. How little I felt in the presence of such a man, so powerful, so apt, so used to this kind of conflict. I took time off for prayer; two words came to my mind which I immediately jotted down in my notebook: be firm, and smile. My adversary began by trying to intimidate me by all kinds of threats and promises. But I had received my marching orders: be firm. I remained inflexible. Exasperated, he let himself throw a tantrum. Then I remembered the second word that I'd received and I calmly kept smiling.

When I was ready to leave, the notary whispered into my ear, "You've won." A few days later, in fact, I received an offer with terms acceptable to both parties. Did my marching orders come from God? Of course I cannot prove such an assertion, but that is what I believe. Faith would no longer be faith if there no longer remained any possibility of doubt. Yes, I believe God can speak to us and lead us more surely than any of our wisest throughts. However, serious conflicts have arisen between me and other friends equally trusting in and seeking divine guidance. This is what humbles us and reveals the depth of the difficulty of our human existence.

Those who do not believe in inspiration from God, and who hold to a moral code, have a much easier life. Those, too, who so naïvely believe in it that they are sure of never erring provided that they note their thoughts during times of meditation. For my part, I believe both that nothing else equals the seeking of God's guidance and that we often err in this matter.

Nothing can contribute more to setting us free from our automatic reactions, our prejudices, and our complexes than divine inspiration, which breaks in upon our mental bookkeeping and upsets all its accounts. Yet, we can never flatter ourselves as being completely available to or possessed by the will of God. All those mechanisms which we have studied and which undermine our logical thought come into play also in our seeking after God. Never are we able to approach him, free from all those determining factors, including our own concept of God, always so small and deformed. We so often mistake our own thought or the pulsations of our subconscious for the leading of God!

No book on theology or ethics, no matter how inspired, can fill the immense gap between our finiteness and the undreamed-of greatness of God. Only Jesus closed the gap, but starting from the other end, by stripping off his divine majesty and putting on our human existence. Only he was able to know ever when to resist and when to surrender. Moreover, this demanded of him the utmost faithfulness in meditation, in fasting, in prayer. This is why Christianity is not so much a body of principles as it is a commitment to his person. By him, in fellowship with him, it is possible for us to receive certain benefits of grace, a few rays of light far more authentic and trustworthy than the whole store of human knowledge.

All we can do is try: try sincerely to live a life guided by God. If we want to be altogether sure of his guidance before beginning, we shall fall back into all the problems we have already described. He who does not dare risk being mistaken about the will of God will never come to know him any better. For it is through obedience, yes, even through our misguided actions, that we find ever greater light. That is, on condition that we are willing to re-examine our actions afterward quite honestly and as in the presence of God. God is ever the Hidden One who reveals himself only through our groping after him.

This is why the churches have so little to say to the

world on the practical carrying out of its business. And even on the practical aspect of church business! In preparing for this book, I called upon a theologian well-known for his competence in the field of ethics. We spent an interesting and agreeable evening talking together. He shared biblical insights with me which we have just been mentioning. While taking leave, he said that he'd expected me to question him on his attitude toward divisive issues in the church. His position in his church is similar to that of a bishop in other churches. He admitted how hard put he is in most conflicts within the church, how hard he finds it to know when he should hold out and when he should compromise. How much more difficult, then, it is for theologians to judge matters outside their own domain: political, economic, or scientific.

It is easily understandable, then, why most churches have withdrawn in recent centuries into the strictly religious domain, the very tendency against which Dr. Müller sought to react by founding the Academy at Bad Boll. Many Christians still hold that the churches must not step out beyond their own religious concerns, that they are not competent enough to discuss the world's problems, and that they risk serious internal divisions if they do so.

Nevertheless, the opposite position, symbolized by the Evangelical Academy, has become general. God is not interested just in theology. He created the world and it is his. His church must exercise an inspired influence over the whole of life, professional, economic, and political. The recent popes, as well, have promulgated encyclicals dealing with these matters, and have instituted the Catholic Action lay-groups which study such problems at their level.

How can we apply our faith to our profession? I speak often with my clients about this, and I sense their tremendous need for guidance. How difficult it is, because we've spent so much time barricading the religious sphere of life from the technical spheres. There remains a great effort to be made before our attitudes will change. This is evident to me in the numerous medical meetings that I attend. There is always interest and sympathy, but never is any real synthesis of science and faith attempted. When we speak of medicine, we can hardly speak of faith, and vice versa.

The World Council of Churches also has constituted a Commission on International Affairs. Churches can well proclaim a few great principles with which everyone agrees, but as soon as it is a question of entering into technical details, it is difficult for them to acquire competence, unanimity among themselves, and the necessary authority to speak usefully to the world. When must we resist and when surrender in the great political, social, or economic problems such as obligatory military service, international conflicts, the liberation of nations, the state-planning of the economy, and yet many more? We find the same debates and the same hesitations in the very bosom of the church as we do in the world.

Indeed, to some the churches seem the most traditional element, the most imbued with prejudice, and the least capable of working out new and boldly imaginative solutions. Yes, the instincts, the unconscious factors examined earlier, play an even more vigorous part in collectivities than they do in individuals. Sacrifices which a man may accept in answering God's call could never be asked of nations or of social classes. With Brunner, we must clearly distinguish between the sphere of love and the sphere of law, which alone can settle social matters.

IX. THE SILENCES OF GOD

THE MORE FERVENT Christians, those who believe most firmly in the possibility and incomparable value of divine guidance, turn in prayer to God in their perplexity. From the depths of our heart we seek his light. We would not despise the help of reason, of science, or of psychoanalysis, but we see their clear limitations. We bring our dilemmas to God, seeking an answer. Must we give in, or must we impose our will? And God, in so many cases, gives no reply.

That is the tragedy of so many believers. With the greatest sincerity, the keenest desire to obey God, with tears and prayers, they can for years ask God about what to do in such and such a situation, without any answer coming. They see no more clearly into their problems than do unbelievers. Yet, there is always a God-given solution. It is, however, virtually always quite different from what we would expect. This is what I learn daily in my consulting room where men bring me their life problems.

This is what I must now try to explain. All these men who come to see me ask questions before which I remain answerless. One man, for example, is stifled in his office by the tyranny of a jealous boss: ought he humbly to accept this daily martyrdom or should he risk his family's security by quitting his position? Even should he find another place, he would lose all benefit of seniority, earned by faithfulness in years of service. He is in the midst of plans to build a modest home, and his wife is overjoyed. All this would have to be given up, but his life is impossible in the office.

Another, a young woman, is dominated by a possessive mother still treating her like a baby. She cannot leave to visit a girlfriend without asking permission, and she must give an account for all of her time. And her mother is so fainthearted! She can see only catastrophe ahead, and gives her humiliating advice which betrays a complete lack of confidence in her daughter's ability to conduct herself. If the daughter shows resistance, the situation degenerates into frightful scenes made all the more upsetting to the daughter because of her mother's heart ailment. But, by giving in to her mother, she is encouraging her settling ever more securely into her despotic power. The mother is divorced, moreover, and does not at all approve of her daughter's happy visits to the remarried father. Must she hide the fact of her visits to him?

Another man let himself drift into an affair. He hardly realizes how it happened. He has guilt feelings all right, more with regard to his children than to his wife. If they ever learned of this! He would like to break off the relationship, but feels it would be cowardly. It would iron out his problems at the price of upsetting terribly his mistress who has shown him such a rich and touching affection. He even fears she may seek revenge. On top of all this, his wife seems suspicious of something: should he confess all to her? He is afraid that she could not take it, for she is very sensitive, being a bit of a spoiled child.

Of course, I could multiply such examples. These men and women are always asking questions unanswerable. They would like me to settle them, to act as the umpire. If I were to give advice, I would strip them of responsibility; I would make minors out of these adults. Moreover, who am I to give advice? Can I ever really know the whole situation or the people involved?

Besides, advice does not work. For example, if a Mr. Fainthearted should ever attempt to defend himself, because he has been so advised, he would do it so awkwardly and hesitantly or else so brutally that he would never win his way. He would thus only draw forth a yet more violent provocation and be obliged to take cover. His defeat would be worse than ever. Here is a mother whose children are quarreling. The elder, a boy, comes to her crying: his sister is taking his toys. "Fend for yourself," she tells him, "instead of crying. You're big enough!" Immediately the boy jumps on his little sister and hits her so hard that the mother has to intervene and protect her, and scold the boy.

What then do we do if the dilemma brought to us is unanswerable and if all advice is useless? Let's take another look at the first of the three cases just mentioned. As long as we discuss only the problem obsessing this man, we shall forever turn around in circles. Nothing will come of it. But then one day, without our ever having thought of it, or knowing how it ever came about, our conversation sidetracked upon some altogether different problems. The smallest matter is sufficient: some insignificant matter, a misunderstanding or an oversight, a shade of judgment which forces us to make a full explanation. Or it may be some humorous incident I have just experienced in my own life and which I relate to him, excusing myself for such a digression.

And there, the whole climate has changed. We no longer discuss his problem; we begin to meet as persons. We discover that we have some common problems, common aspirations, and certain indefinable but deep *rapport*. This is called "transference" and "countertransference" by the scientists, and I will not argue with them. What is really important is that something takes place, both in me and in him.

Is this still a matter of psychology? I believe it is more than that, for it is no longer a technical, objective, or scientific matter. It is a quite subjective thing for both people; it is a human and spiritual event. We are no longer the same to each other as we were before. A powerful bond between us has come into existence. The man is less alone than before, less fearful. From then on he becomes less obsessed by his dilemma; he can now talk about many other matters with me. He has found not just affection, but a certain communion with another human being, communion for which all men thirst.

Quite unnoticeably to himself, his attitude in life changes. He thinks that the other people are changing. A child, when it grows up, thinks that the world is shrinking. Unexpectedly, the tyrannical office boss, who so stifled my client, now opens up to him about his own problems, problems he'd never dreamed existed. My client is absolutely amazed! He begins to understand why his boss has been so jealous because he is beginning to know something of his personal life. He is beginning to know of the other's great sufferings.

Thus a sympathetic bond is created between the boss and the employee who used to detest him, a bond which will transform the atmosphere of the whole office. A few days earlier such a development would have seemed unimaginable to either of them. Then suddenly the whole dilemma disappears! "Must I suffer in silence or must I walk out and slam the door?" It is no longer a question of either. The problem is solved because the men have changed.

A similar adventure was experienced by the young woman with the possessive mother. She would have had her mother change in her attitude, but did not know what approach to follow in order to gain. I could give her no answer for that. But then, after having opened up to me about many other much more personal and confidential matters, and after having cried about them, she began to feel less weighed-down. She was no longer torn between her parents because she was changing herself, growing up. Then one day she told me she had begun to pray again, and realized that she had not been right with God because she'd held it against him for leaving her helpless in such a hopeless situation. And then, all of a sudden, she discovered that her mother had begun to respect her. By some strange reversal of roles, it is now the mother who seeks advice of her daughter. She senses a strength which she herself lacks, and which has banished her daughter's fears.

What of the unfaithful husband? He is quite capable of discovering his own weakness to be the cause of tension in both his wife and his mistress. Deep down he was no more than a child seeking approval and consolation, and not realizing the consequences of his own actions. When a man is weak, the women around him are anxious. This man found that both his mistress and his wife were able to cope with the painful straightening out of the situation as soon as he showed manly courage and firm decisiveness.

Life problems are not like algebraic equations, which can be turned in every way, all over the page, until the final answer $x=25$ is worked out at the bottom. The situation of a life problem is always dependent upon a new awakening of the conscience, a change in attitude, a growth in personality. It may come through psychoanalysis or through reading the Bible; the phenomenon is the same. The insoluble dilemmas thus give way. The boss no longer has to wonder whether he should impose his will upon his subordinates in order to maintain order, nor to give in so as to develop their initiative and experience. He has acquired a new authority with them which saves him both from having to smash his fist down on the table and from pretending not to see anything.

It is in the form of alternatives that our problems first appear to us. We cannot formulate problems in any other than intellectual language. Now the property of intellectual language is its dilemma—either this or that—either I fight or I surrender. The one seems to exclude the other. The intellect reasons about a situation as if it were fixed and unchangeable. But what escapes intelligence is life itself, movement, change in people which changes the given elements of the problem and which tears us from the prison-grasp of the syllogism. Then, resistance and surrender no longer are opposites; one can both fight and compromise, so to speak, at the same time. Rather, he no longer needs either to give in or to fight on in the way he imagined before.

In the same way that my clients bring their problems to my consultation room, we all press our problems upon God. It is precisely in our moments of meditation and seeking for divine guidance that we do this. We should like to force him into settling the issue, oblige him to give an answer. And he remains silent! We fail to see that by our thus asking God questions, even in the reverence of prayer, we are still attempting to remain in charge of our meditation rather than let God direct us.

At the very time that we are asking questions of God, questions which remain unanswered, he is ever asking other questions which we fail to heed. Yes, questions altogether different, which we elude, because we know what obedience would cost us. We know what should be changed in our lives, that which is nobody's responsibility but our own. Let us open the Bible—it is clearly evident from one end to the other. Men throw out questions to God which remain unanswered. But they change, and find unexpected solutions when they begin to listen to the questions God asks of them, and to answer him. Jesus did not answer the weighted questions of his contradictors; he always asked them other questions, embarrassing ones, capable of making them take stock of themselves.

The book of Job is a striking example. Job, in the midst of undeserved suffering, shouts to God, barraging him with countless "Why's?" The book ends without God ever having answered. Thus the problem of unjust suffering has remained unresolved all through these centuries, that is, in its form of a syllogism over which all logical minds stumble: either God is all-powerful and therefore unjust, or else he is just but not all-powerful. Job, however, received his answer—an altogether different kind. It was not an intellectual reply, but an experience of God, once he paid attention to the questions God was asking. The philosophical problem of unjust suffering remains unsolved, but Job's attitude completely altered because he met God: "I had heard of thee by the hearing of the ear, but now my eye sees thee" (Job 42:5). As long as men remain in a strictly intellectual frame of mind, they will always brandish their problems as so many challenges to which no satisfactory answer has come.

X. THE PERSONAL LEVEL

THERE ARE, then, two distinct levels: the level of logic and reason, of dilemma, of all our insoluble questions and problems. Then there is the deeper level of the personal, of life, of a living and personal encounter with God and with men. The solution of our problems is to be found always on the deeper level. Just as precious as reason is, in solving technical and scientific problems, it is powerless to settle the problems of life.

Not only is reason powerless; far worse, it is dangerous. For the end result of every logical dilemma, conflict of ideas or conflict of feelings, is to shut us up in an immovable position. It seems to be a strong position, unanswerable and triumphant; it permits us to throw out our challenges and to reduce to silence all those who would try to give us advice. Oh, how dangerous it is to be right and to be sure of it! We can no longer change or modify our viewpoint.

On the other hand, by abandoning our intellectual defense, by going down to the deeper, personal level, by coming to see what we have not yet understood of the mysteries of life, and by willingly coming to see ourselves as we really are, with our real problems, we always enter into an experience fruitful and renewing.

60

Let us take the most common of problems, that of the unmarried woman who suffers atrociously from being unmarried and from the rebellion which it produces in her. Must she accept it as the very will of God and renounce her perfectly natural desire for marriage? Is it not the legitimate hope of every woman, except those who may feel called to remain celibate? On the other hand, is she to fight against it, to pray and cry out to heaven above, to use all her wits at the risk of only aggravating her suffering further? Is she finally to marry just any other man, as her friends seem to be suggesting when they tell her that the reason she hasn't married is that she's too choosy? She may change her mind ceaselessly, from the one attitude to the other without ever knowing which is right. She may pray without ever receiving an answer from God. A day may come when she will see that the two possibilities are not so contradictory as she thought, that she can surrender to God and leave her life and her destiny in his hands without in any way giving up the struggle or even her own legitimate desires. Far from it, for the struggle is far more effective if she is freed from all feeling of self-pity or bitterness.

We discover a similar process throughout the most differing types of problems. Here are parents whose daughter had fallen in love with a man they felt could never make her happy. Could they remain passive when they could only see a life of suffering ahead for her? Should they put pressure on her, exercise their authority, threaten her, and thus risk driving her, through despair, into the arms of her suitor? I had no answer to give them. But there were many other questions which these parents might well ask of themselves, deep reflection they might well make upon their past actions, and attempt a drastic review of their relationship with their daughter all through her youth. And now, a full year afterward, they have written that their daughter broke off with her suitor, and is now married to a man whom they were able to welcome joyfully; their daughter is happy.

Thus the solution of a problem always demands that we descend to a deeper level. We must leave the level of conflicts and dilemmas to the level of self-examination under the searching light of God. We then can understand that a dilemma is a sign; it is a sign that there are deeper discoveries to be made, a new order to perceive which will transform the whole nature of the problem.

The new order is the very thing which the New Testament calls the Kingdom of Heaven. You cannot enter therein, said Jesus, "unless your righteousness exceeds that of the scribes and Pharisees" (Matt. 5:20). Scribal righteousness is that of logic, casuistry, dilemma, captious questions, and dialectic.

True meditation is this descent to the deeper level under God's direction. There it is that really new inspirations come, to set us free from our dilemmas, to transform our relationships with ourselves, with others, with God. Under every dilemma is hidden several fears: the fear of openly resisting, the fear of giving in, the fear of fighting, and the fear of being beaten. It is love which drives back fear.

All is not thus solved. Every day we shall find ourselves before the most perplexing questions, even if we sincerely seek for divine guidance. Yet, these can each be for us an opportunity for deeper, inner experience through which alternatives we thought to be incompatible may be resolved in new synthesis. We used to set doubt in opposition to faith, acceptance to rebellion, self-affirmation to self-surrender, and resistance to giving in. We do so no longer.

Here it is that real life always unites into a marvelous harmony those movements of the inner person which we judged to be contradictory. They are shown to be only complementary. The real believer is not the man who hides from himself those persistent doubts

deep down but irremovable. The opposite is the truth:
"I believe; help my unbelief!" (Mark 9:24). The
strong man is not he who hides his own failings from
himself, but he who knows them well. Surrendering our
life to God is at the same time our supreme giving-in
and our supreme act of self-affirmation!

The theme of this work is that dilemma which faces
us every day in a thousand different ways: to resist or
to surrender? It is clear that the distinction which we
now must maintain, distinction between the two different levels at which problems may be solved, is of
very general application. There are many purely scientific and technical problems which can be solved by
these disciplines. However, there are other problems
which elude every attempt at objective solution. These
latter are thus signs, on the plane of our intellectual
consciousness, of deeper and more hidden problems
which can be resolved only at another level, that of
personal and spiritual life, that is, on the personal level.

Therapy of the person is not just another remedy,
something (like a prayer, for example) which we pre-
scribe instead of digitalis or electro-shock. It means
going down to another level which implies an altogether different kind of personal commitment from the
doctor. Thanks to this the patient may be enabled to
discover deeper problems within himself which have
played a part in his sickness. He may also be enabled
to grow into a greater personal maturity so that the
given elements of his health situation may themselves
change.

The churches can help men from every profession,
and through them, the nations of our world, by carefully studying their problems, by meditating on them
before God, and by bringing the light of God's revelation upon them. But the churches can help our world
even more, by supplying that which is missing, this new
dimension of the personal at which level those difficul-

ties which escape reason, science, and technical skill
can yet be worked out.

It seems to me, then, that there are three stages in
our search for behavior-direction. First, there is that of
logical thought, which draws up every problem as a dilemma—it is to be settled then, as wisely as possible,
using all the help available from science, moral consciousness, clear analysis of the situation, and depth
psychology.

There is also the stage at which divine guidance is
sought. It is still pursued at the level of dilemmas, but
it seeks a solution to these dilemmas either by discovering God's answer through an objective study of the
biblical revelation and of theological doctrine, or else
by a direct and subjective enlightenment experienced
through meditation and prayer. Clearly, this stage of
seeking is valid only for believers.

The third stage is found at the deeper level, that of
personal growth which bypasses the dilemma, that of a
change in the person himself which conforms to God's
plan. It leads him into the integration of contradictory
tendencies which hitherto were tearing him apart. It is
the entry into the deeper level which is called in the
Bible *metanoia*. Such an experience is by no means re-
served only for believers. It is of universal application.
Certainly, it is of God's grace, but as Jesus said, God
"makes his sun rise on the evil and on the good"
(Matt. 5:45).

Those of us who believe know that the sun comes
from God, as do the rain, the growth of flowers, the
birth of the person and his maturing. We know the
source, in God's love. We can help others to experience
it even if they do not know God. Perhaps through this
experience they can be helped toward a personal encounter with God, the Author and Finisher of all.